Food For The Spirit

Spirit

A 21 Day Journey of Spiritual Growth

Food For The Spirit

A 21 Day Journey of Spiritual Growth

Bilon Joseph

JAMA
Publishing
Newberry,Florida 32669

FOOD FOR THE SPIRIT
Bilon Joseph
Copyright © 2014 by Sherman and Bilon Joseph
Published by JAMA Publishing
Gainesville, Florida 32669

Visit our Web site at www.jamapublishing.com

JAMA is an imprint of JAMA Publishing.
The JAMA name and logo are trademarks of JAMA Publishing, Inc.

Printed in the United States of America

First Edition: April 2014
10 9 8 7 6 5 4 3 2 1

ISBN 978-0-9960793-0-3

To the people who pushed me when I didn't want to be pushed; to the people who supported me and sacrificed with me, I am grateful to God for you. This book would not be possible without your inspiration and your faith in me. You, in turn, helped me to have faith in myself and in my God-given abilities. This gift is no longer mine to hoard all to myself; I now gift it to my dear reader. Sherman, Maya, and Jacqueline, I love you! And to God Almighty I dedicate this gift to you!

Bilon

Table of Contents

Why 21?

It has been said that it takes 21 days of consistently doing something to form a new habit. Whether adapting to a healthier lifestyle, learning to be on time, or not hitting the snooze button incessantly, three weeks of consistently making or breaking a habit is believed to make this change permanent.

As Christians, it should be our ultimate goal to walk, talk, and become like Christ. In other words, we should desire to grow! Spiritual growth is not that dissimilar from physical growth in that growth is vital to health and life. Without growth, all things and anything will die. Without maturation, development is stunted, and our purpose can never be fully realized. You see, once you are saved, your spirit belongs to God, but your mind...? Now that needs a makeover!

Romans 12:1 encourages us to be transformed by the renewing of our minds. We renew our minds by changing our thinking. One thought at a time, we learn who God is, who He declares we are; and when we actually start believing this truth enough to apply it to every aspect of our lives, everything changes.

Living Life on Purpose

God doesn't want us to live life lackadaisically. I believe God doesn't want us to live life without direction, aimlessly wondering from one moment to the next. I can safely assume this because of the mere fact that He kept our beautiful Savior, Jesus, His *only* begotten son, in reserve as a lamb already slain before the foundations of the universe! This clearly demonstrates that God Almighty is a planner! Everything He has created has a purpose, a plan to be fulfilled during its time here on this earth.

Everything has a purpose. Every plant has a system within itself that works to develop and sustain life. Every insect has a function. Although they may pester us from time to time, the world without them would be a maddening place. Without honey bees and their ability to pollinate, some flowers could not reproduce! Could you imagine no flowers in the springtime? Without flowers, there would be less oxygen to breathe. Indeed, every living and non-living thing on this planet has a divine purpose, a reason for being! How much more you and I, who God took the time to mold by His own hands and breathe His breath of life into? How much more *you* His son or daughter?

Freedom Found in Surrender

Spiritual growth gives you and I the desire to not only exchange our stinking thinking for the divine thoughts of the Creator himself, but it gives us the desire to love God, love His people, and live life the way He originally planned, purposed, and designed for our lives to be lived! This is what I believe Christ meant when he said that "The thief comes only to steal and kill and destroy; I have come that they may have **life**, and have it more abundantly." (John 10:9-10).

So, again, Why 21?

Food for the Spirit: 21 Days of Spiritual Growth has been intentionally designed to assist you in your personal journey to grow spiritually! Spiritual growth requires time: time in prayer, time studying the word, and time applying the word to our lives. In a culture that is busy being busy, we may not be investing the time to grow because we believe we don't have the time to do so. Or for some of us, we want to grow but do not exactly know where to begin. This book is for you!

For twenty-one days we will take the journey together to begin creating a new habit. For twenty one days we will commit to setting aside a few minutes, literally, to consciously spend time with the Creator of the Universe! Together, we will take one step closer to God and one step closer to which we are destined to be: believers walking, talking, and breathing in the fullness of Christ as **mature** Christians! With this understood, we can be confidant that beginning this journey closer to God will in turn draw Him closer to us! How magnificent is that?

Twenty-one days of thinking what God thinks, meditating on what God says, and applying what God says is sure to produce something epic in your hearts and in your lives! It is my prayer that the next twenty one days will be the beginning of something absolutely amazing as you grow spiritually.

What to Expect?

But the fruit of the Spirit is love, joy, peace, patience, kindness, goodness,
faithfulness, gentleness, and self-control.
Against such things there is no law.
Galatians 5:22-23

W
hat you *won't* find in this book is your typical devotional: a scripture and a very didactic interpretation of that scripture.

Instead, *Food for the Spirit* is a book purposely designed to edify your spirit! This book will expound on the living word of God, and will challenge you with practical tools and strategies to take your life and your spiritual journey to the next level!

Consider this twenty one day journey as a partnership that you and I are agreeing to undertake, together. My job is to give you the word, show you how to apply that word, and coach you through actually walking the word out in your everyday life.

One week at a time for three weeks, we will concentrate on three attributes of the fruit of the spirit: love, joy, and peace. I'm going to provide you with some purpose-filled scriptures that we will use as our motivation to learn, understand, and apply what God says about love, joy, and peace to our everyday lives. This process will allow us to begin seeing the growth and the change that we truly desire to have in our lives.

Each chapter will include seven devotionals dedicated to that week's attribute. Each devotional includes a practical interpretation, a What Does God Say scripture, and a Food for the Spirit Dessert; and at the end of each chapter, there will be Work My Faith life application tools.

What Does God Say

Every day we are inundated with messages. We then internalize these messages, whether from television, movies, or the internet, and we accept them as truth. We begin to believe that we should look a certain way, that we should have so much, and that we should be so far along in our careers, our relationships, and the like. And much of this information is misinformation working to keep us spinning our wheels, frustrated and deceived.

Remember, I explained earlier that spiritual growth begins with a renewed mind, and a renewed mind is a transformed mind. We have to change our thinking before growth or change can occur. To assist us in this process, for the next twenty one days we will exchange one of these faulty thoughts for what God says about the matter!

The What Does God Say scripture will be our guide post for each day's devotion. These are the scriptures that we will mediate on daily and will want to begin committing to memory. These are the scriptures that we want to write on sticky notes and post on our mirrors, on the inside of the front door, on our cubicles at work, or wherever we can see it and read it on a regular basis.

Food for the Spirit Dessert

Once you have fed your spirit with the main course, I've provided you with some additional scriptures to further delve into the theme of that day's devotional! This gives you the opportunity to continue to meditate on scriptures that will build your faith and will encourage you to activate that word into your lives immediately!

Work My Faith

At the end of each chapter, there will be a Work My Faith resource. This tool will help you take what God says and begin to actively apply it to your life NOW. Without faith it impossible to please God (Hebrews 11:6), but faith without works is dead (James 2:20)! It is not enough to say: "I believe God's word to be true", but never take Him at His word to actually apply it to our everyday lives. If we believe, which I know we do, we have to actively put the word to work!

Putting our faith to action will be the determining factor of how much or how effectively we will begin or continue to grow spiritually. To accomplish this task, our strategies will include:

- Journaling
- Self-work Assignments
- Exercises/ Activities

I would recommend you begin keeping a journal to help you record your progress, your thoughts, and your experiences throughout our journey.

I believe, whole-heartedly, that as you set apart time for God and with God, you will begin to see things in your lives dramatically change for the better. And as you begin putting the word into daily practice, by the end of this twenty one day journey, I know that you will experience a greater level of love, joy, and peace in your hearts and in your lives.

I thank you for allowing me to take this journey of changing the course of your entire life right alongside you. I am excited about your spiritual growth and you're establishing a deeper intimacy with Christ. And more importantly, I am delighted about your Day 22 and beyond!

Week 1: Love

To begin cultivating the attribute of love in our hearts, we need to first have a clear understanding of what love is. Biblically speaking, there are several translations for the word love. If I show love to my brother, this love in the Greek is *phileo* which means brotherly love. Phileo would not be the same love I would display to my husband. This love, *philandros*, is a romantic love.

Regardless of the term or translation I use, all love, *true* love, stems from the same source, God! The dictionary defines love in a variety of ways, but the one that pertained to *agape* love, that is, the love the Father has for us, is defined as this: an unselfish loyal and benevolent concern for the good of another.

God's love or this *agape* love is an action and is displayed through selflessness and commitment. Consider how God revealed His love to the world. God's love for this world moved Him to do the most unselfish act imaginable: He sent from the wonders of Heaven His regal Son into a dying, sinful, and dark world. If that wasn't enough, God then wrapped Christ's divinity in humanity so that He would experience ALL that His creation endured in this flesh! He then allowed His creation, to judge, condemn, humiliate, brutally beat beyond recognition, spit upon, and mock.

If this wasn't enough, He then allowed Jesus to carry a rugged, heavy cross of shame down a crowded path to ultimately be nailed, both hands and feet, to a cross for this *same* creation! Still not enough, His beloved Son dies and three day later rises from death. All for love… all for His love for us… and all because that's who He is!

Love, defined a part from God, cannot be defined as such, for God is indeed love. The apostle John reminds us in 1 John 4: 8 that "Whoever does not love does not know God, because God is love." As Christians, it should be our ultimate desire to grow in love because God is love. Our love for God will naturally create an indelible desire within us to love others with the same love that He first demonstrated to us through Christ's example on the cross.

Now, please understand, I am not telling you that you must be crucified to display your love for others as Christ did. I am saying that real love, God's love is unselfish, and it's reserved for the good of others. This is often the difficult part to accept and duplicate in our everyday lives.

We live in a "me, myself, and I" society that will seldom promote service, selflessness, and compassion. It promotes much of the opposite. We are inferentially and explicitly taught that we must go about life "getting what belongs to us" at any costs because we deserve to be happy…Christ's message is extremely contrary to our cultural norms.

Nevertheless, when we receive God's love, His love begins to revolutionize our souls! His love begins to melt our hearts so that we are now able to love what He loves and to love how He loves. For this reason, I do not think it a coincidence that love is listed as the first attribute of the Fruit of the Spirit.

Without God's love, we cannot love Him in return, we cannot love ourselves, and we cannot love others. Without Christ's love in our hearts through the power of His most Holy Spirit, we won't desire His will or His way, and there would then be no need to cultivate His fruit in our lives. Love is certainly the foundation that our faith, Christianity, is built upon. Without the love of Christ in our hearts, Christianity in its purist form does not exist…

With this being understood, we need God's love **overflowing** in our hearts! It is His love that will begin to change us from the inside out, and it will be His love flowing through us that will light up this dark world! So, without further ado, let us begin cultivated this awesome attribute: *love*!

Day 1: Fire Burning Within!

What Does God Say?
Blessed are those who hunger and thirst for righteousness,
for they will be filled.
Matthew 5:6

I gave my life to Christ, officially, at eighteen. I remember how excited I was to be forgiven and to be made new! God had undoubtedly touched my life, and His Holy Spirit was living within me! I felt like someone had given me the most refreshing shower that I'd ever experienced in life. I felt new… I felt clean… I was born again!

Naturally, I was beyond excited! I wanted the whole world to know about this wonderful experience that had just taken place in my life. I wanted everyone I knew and didn't know to experience this amazing love that I'd discovered when I said *Yes* to Christ!

I delved into the Bible, soaking up everything I could learn and memorize. I joined a wonderful ministry and served anywhere I could serve. I prayed as often as possible. I fasted weekly! I was leading people to Christ on a consistent basis! I was on FIRE! But you can imagine what happened over time. All of my innocent zeal soon became watered down by experience and time.

Going Through the Motions

What happened? How did I go from on fire to lukewarm? Life happened, I got busy, and I spent less time with God and with His word without even realizing it. I continued to go to church, and I continued to serve, but, even with all of my righteous acts, I had fallen away from God. I knew His word... I knew the order of service, and I knew the latest gospel songs. I knew when to smile... I could finish the famous church colloquialisms without thought (God is good all the time, and all the time God is good); I could judge and critique with the best of them: I saw someone else's splinter and unknowingly ignored the beam in my own! I had become intellectually obese with sermon after sermon after sermon! On the surface, I was no longer hungry, but spiritually, I was emaciated...

Down by the Riverside

Until...one day, a little over a year ago, I came near a river. Have you ever been near a beach, a bay, a creek, or some other body of water? I mean, you can't see the water, but you can smell it. You can feel it. The temperature begins to change as you get closer to it, so much so, that you can feel this same water that you still cannot see! When I came near this river, something awoke inside of me, and I begin to question, "There has to be more to Christianity than this?" It was in this moment, that my stomach started to growl and my mouth began to grow dry.

I wanted to have real joy! I needed peace. I didn't have victory in my marriage, in my parenting, on my job, in my finances. In fact, I was defeated. It was as if I had been on this spiritual rollercoaster: up one day, down the next, and I was more than ready to get off once and for all!

At this point, I know you are wondering, "What does this have to do with love?" God is love, remember? So where can we find *real* love? Only in Him and only with Him! You see, love begins to develop in our hearts the more time we spend with Love, God!

Our hunger and thirst for God will draw us to Him. And when that happens, the fire returns or never leaves if you are diligent! The compassion that this love brings rules in your heart!

Will you be able to love the unlovable, the annoying, or the frustrating right away? No. Will you miss the mark at times? Yes! But we keep going forward, deeper and deeper into the person and the presence of God until we reach the place where love is matured and running over in our lives.

Dear Jesus,
*Give us a renewed hunger and thirst for your presence, for your beautiful Word, for your power. As we spend time with you, Lord, teach us to love the lovable **and** the unlovable. Forgive us when we miss the mark, and thank you for giving us the power to love through your most Holy Spirit.*

In Your Name We Pray,
Amen

Food for the Spirit Dessert
John 4:14; John 6:48-51; Psalms 42:1-2

Day 2: A Love Worth Dying For

What Does God Say?

Very truly I tell you, unless a kernel of wheat falls to the ground and dies, it remains only a single seed. But if it dies, it bears much fruit.
John 12:24

Selfish people find it extremely difficult to love anyone other than themselves, and even that love is questionable. How do I know? I have spent a good portion of my life being unknowingly selfish, entitled, and self-motivated. What do I mean when I say unknowingly? Well, I thought that everything I did was justifiable. I had an excuse or a good reason for it all. I wanted my way. My instinct was to get what I wanted, and if that meant manipulating you until I got it, then I was willing to do that. In short, it was all about me, me, and a little more me!

Die to Live

Maybe your selfish tendencies are not as blatant as mine were. Perhaps you do not like to share. Perhaps you pass the homeless vagrant on the street instead of obliging him/her by giving a few dollars or buying them a meal. Maybe you are impatient and want what you want exactly when you want it.

Whatever your vice may be, it is next to impossible to begin cultivating love in a heart that is congested with selfishness. This is where that "dying" thing comes in. When we begin to love like God loves, we have to die! Not a literal death, but definitely a spiritual one.

Tying God's Hands

As long as you and I are motivated by what will give us the glory, we are tying God's hands. Those same tied hands now have no room to work on our hearts. But when we take our eyes off of ourselves and place them on God and His will for our lives, love has room to grow.

As I began to spend more time with God, little by little, He began to clean up my heart. Like an expert farmer, He was able to now till the soil of my heart, breaking up the stony ground so that the fruit of His Spirit could grow healthy and strong there.

This process has taught and is teaching me (I am a work in progress. We all are!) how to love what He loves. My consistent prayer is "Lord, give me a heart like yours!" He will teach us how to love when we die to our selfish desires and to our limited understanding. In other words, our surrender is key. And let me tell you, my heart has become tenderer with each passing day. I am moved by what moves the heart of Christ. I am filled with compassion to serve instead of waiting to be served. I am learning that it doesn't have to be all about me, and that it is wonderful to make every day and every moment of my life all... about... Jesus!

Dear Jesus,

We surrender our will and our faulty ways to you today. We lay our lives down and pick up true life that is only found in you. Lord, give us a heart like yours. Give us a clean heart that we may cheerfully serve you and others. We love you God, and we thank you for your unfailing love that keeps us and guides us daily.

In Your Name We Pray,
Amen

Food for the Spirit Dessert

1 Corinthians 15: 36-38; 1 Corinthians 1:4; Hebrews 2: 9-10

Day 3: I Choose to Love

What Does God Say?

Love is patient, love is kind. It does not envy,
it does not boast, it is not proud.
1 Corinthians 13:4

This is probably one of the most recognizable scriptures about love next to John 3:16 in the entire Bible. I have probably heard this scripture recited more times than I can count, especially when I attended someone's wedding. In fact, this scripture was used as a part of my own wedding ceremony.

I remember hearing my husband's grandfather read this passage in his thick Costa Rican accent from a small, black leather-bound Bible. The words seemed to leap from the page, piercing me with the magnitude and its beauty and its truth! In such an emotional moment, vows and any recitation that might occur are so heartfelt because they are recited in **emotion!**

What a Feeling!

I don't know about you, but when I am emotional, everything, and I mean *everything*, I say, do, and think is over- the- top or exaggerated. I am not really counting the costs or weighing the matter because I am enraptured with emotion. There is no logical or rational thought process occurring. I am reacting out of the wellspring of my feelings. And maybe your feelings aren't this way, but my feelings fluctuate! They are up one moment and down the next, so if I allow my life to be led by my emotions or by my feelings, I would be certifiably insane! I would be diagnosed with somebody's something and ready for a stray- jacket because I absolutely could not function within my feelings on a consistent basis.

It's Up To You

This is why I believe true love cannot be emotional! If it was, we would love someone today and hate that same someone tomorrow. Love has more substance than that. Love requires more than a fleeting feeling. Love, true love, takes time and takes work. A lot of it!

As believers, we want to learn love, and we want to practice this love in our lives each and every day. Love will teach us to be patient with ourselves and with others as we all endure the process of becoming our best selves. Love will teach us to be kind even when we feel kindness is not deserved or has not been earned. Love will teach us to celebrate one another and not covet or be jealous of each other. Love will teach us a quiet confidence and true humility. Love, when cultivated, will permeate every area of our lives within and without as we become more intimate with the author of love, God Almighty!

Do you choose to embrace love and all of the responsibilities that are attached to it? Will you chose to give love when you don't feel like it or it doesn't benefit you to do so? This love that causes patience, kindness, and humility to bloom in our hearts will cost us everything. Beloved, will you choose to love?

Dear Jesus,

It is difficult to love when love is not returned in the same measure. It is hard to love when we are frustrated with those who we are required to love, but, Lord, you love us even when we don't deserve it, return it, or consider it. Teach us to extend this same grace as we love others.

In Your Name We Pray,
Amen

Food for the Spirit Dessert

Proverbs 10:12; Ephesians 4:32; Ecclesiastes 7:8-9

Day 4: Oh, How He Loves Us!

What Does God Say?

For God so loved the world that he gave his one and only Son, that whoever believes in him shall not perish but have eternal life.

John 3:16

Thanks to Tim Tebow, many are familiar with this verse. He was famous for it being inked beneath his eyelids during Gator football games.

This same scripture is often recited during the Offering in a Sunday morning service. Pastors, deacons, ministers, and the like, place great emphasis on the fact that God demonstrated His love for all of mankind by the act of **giving**! They go on to explain that because God's love moved Him to give what was most precious to Him—His son, Jesus—we too should demonstrate our love for God by giving what is most precious to us, our money.

No matter where you have heard this scripture, if you have even heard this scripture at all, it holds so much power. And the power, I would agree, is made known through the act of giving! Love and giving should go hand in hand. When we love someone or something we are willing to do almost anything or pay almost everything to obtain the object of our affection.

Love with Stipulations

Just remember your first love. You were head over hills. Your *love* was like fireworks on the Fourth of the July. No one could tell you anything to contest what you were feeling. Every day you had butterflies in your stomach, sweaty palms, and you floated in anticipation until you could talk to, hear from, or simply be around the love of your life!

This infatuation acted as the heart's blind fold, allowing us to overlook any of our love's flaws or wayward behavior. Everything was adorable, beautiful, wonderful! Until the emotions wore off and you came crashing down from euphoria.

No longer blind, you were able to see that Romeo wasn't always chivalrous. You were able to see that Juliet wasn't always as sweet as pie, and the *love* that you just knew you were in dissipated...

A Love We Could Never Earn

Now, consider our Heavenly Father! He sees our flaws. He is intimate with our issues. He is aware of the multitudes of sins we've participated in. He sees us raw, uncovered, and without makeup, yet the love He has for mankind, for this world, didn't dissipate. In fact, it grew! It grew to the extent that He accepted that the *only* way to save this dying world that He loved so dearly was to **give** what was most precious and most valuable to Him, His only begotten son, Jesus Christ!

Show me someone who will give their best and their last to someone or for someone who cannot or will not do the same in return, and I will show you someone who is **in** love! This love is selfless. It is not concerned about its well- being but only about the well- being of the one it loves.

Qualified by Love

This is the love God desires in return. We have to want to give everything to Christ: our hearts, our souls, our lives, our money, our time...everything! Why? Because He is the only one worth giving this agape love to. He deserves it!

But before we can give this type of love to God, we have to be willing to receive that His love made us worthy to be loved in such a manner. No matter what we have done, no matter where we have been, God wants us to receive the truth that Jesus loves us. We can't earn it, we will never deserve it, but He is head over the hills, cow over the moon in love with us! Will you receive this love today?

Dear Jesus,

Thank you for your love. Thank you for the sacrifice you made so that we can experience your love in our lives. Help us to receive your love, a love that we didn't have to nor could ever earn. Teach us to offer you the love you deserve in every area of our lives. To you we give ourselves away!

In Your Name We Pray,
Amen

Food for the Spirit Dessert
Romans 8:32; 1 John 4:9-10

Day 5: A Love Revolution

What Does God Say?
If you love those who love you, what reward will you get?
Are not even the tax collectors doing that?
Matthew 5:46

L et me begin by saying, "Ouch!" How easy it is—most of the time—to love our family members, our friends, and the everyday people that we have some sort of positive relationship with? These are the people whose love and loyalty have been tested, tried, and true. They are the ones who know you like no other. They are often the ones that accept you when the world may not. Even when you "fall out", after the smoke has cleared, you still love them, and they still love you. Easy.

The Unlovables

Conversely, maybe you come from a family that was not easy to love, or you may feel they did not love you in return. I would counter that there was someone in your life: a teacher, a neighbor, a guidance counselor, a significant other, or a BFF (best friend forever) who loved and supported you! They understood you, and they were there for you when you needed them. Again, these are the people who we love with ease.

But what about the unlovables? You know, the overbearing boss, the inconsiderate neighbor, the gossiping co-worker, the driver that cuts you off, the child that steps on your toe, the ex that broke your heart, the parent that was missing in action...Do we love them? Do we even think about loving them? Naturally, why would we? They've hurt us...they've caused us immense frustration...they don't deserve our love, right?

Sweet Surrender

Trust me, I hear your frustration, and I feel your pain. I am in the trenches with you! However, for as unnatural and as uncomfortable as it may be, we have to love *everyone*: both the lovable and the not quite so lovable.

This feat will only be accomplished through the power of the Holy Spirit! In our own strength and in our own ability, we simply are not capable of this rainbows, sunshine, and blue skies kind of love. We need the Lord for this one! We desperately need the love of God to saturate us beyond measure on the inside until it overflows on the outside to *everyone*!

How does this happen? Surrender. You have to be willing to surrender your will to God. Surrendering your old thought system that says you should hate those who harm you; this simply is not the gospel. Christ called us to love those who spitefully use us. I mean, in the mist of hanging from the cross that He was nailed to, in agony, in pain, and grieved, Jesus asked that God the Father would forgive His tormentors, for they didn't know what they were doing!

Transformation

Cultivating love in our hearts, believe it or not, will transform us to be able to love in this manner. The same Spirit that filled Christ Jesus on this earth and rose Him from the dead, is the very same Spirit that lives in you and me. That means we have that same power to forgive and to love in spite of, just like Jesus does! That's good news!

Will this divine, agape love, develop within our hearts over night? No, not in most cases, I assume. But can this type of agape love radically revolutionize our hearts and our lives? Most definitely! How do we begin? Congratulations, you are taking the first step right now! You are well on your way!

Dear Jesus,

Thank you for loving us first! Thank you for loving us, the once unlovable. We seek more of you! May we be ever transformed by your Spirit, your presence, your power, and your LOVE! We love you and help us to begin sharing that love with the world!

In Your Name We Pray,
Amen

Food for the Spirit Dessert

Luke 6:32-35; Matthew 5:47-48

Day 6: We Are Family!

What Does God Say?

A new commandment I give to you, that you love one another, even as I have loved you, that you also love one another. By this all men will know that you are My disciples, if you have love for one another.
John 13:34-35

In my years of being a Christian, I have spent a lot of time in church and around church people. For every church I have attended, there has been a fair amount of people who were very loving and who were very kind. Likewise, there have been a fair amount of very mean and messy people within those same four walls.

Now, I have come to learn that people are as varied inside of the church as they are outside of it. I do not allow the misconduct or the attitude of one person in the church to sour my entire perspective of the church as a whole. Church is a hospital where sick, bound, sinful people come to be healed, set-free, and redeemed!

Commanded to Love

In these beautiful verses, Christ gave us a new command-ment. To be clear, a commandment is not a suggestion. It is mandatory. With this understood, God clearly commands us, His disciples, to love one another.

In the New Testament, the first Christians were a family. They spent time with each other, a lot of time! They prayed for each other. They met one another's needs. No one experienced lack. Whether Jew or Gentile, bond or free... as a fellow believer, the Christians took care of and had compassion for one another. They were united. They were one! In fact, this is how Christians earned the name "Christian". The love they displayed to each other was so similar to the love Christ had shown to His disciples and to others that non-believers started referring to them as Christians or little Jesus'.

I Need You, You Need Me

With this understood, the myth that we can be followers of Christ on our own is dispelled. In truth, being a Christian means that we have been grafted into a body of believers—each one having a different function but all having the same purpose: to be the hands and feet of Jesus.

We are family. God desires for us, his sons and daughters, to be there for one another through prayer, word of encouragement, patience, service, and the like. When we support and forgive one another, we are pleasing God and following His commandment!

Love amongst Christians regardless of denomination, race, and so one has the power to represent Christ so appropriately on this earth! What a privilege to be a part of a community of people who love God and who love one another!

Dear Jesus,

We pray for unity amongst Christians all over this world. May we not focus on what makes us different, but, instead, teach us to embrace and celebrate who makes us the same, You. Teach us to work together for the common good of honoring you, spreading the gospel of Christ, and serving those in need.

In Your Name We Pray,
Amen

Food for the Spirit Dessert
Leviticus 19:18; Ephesians 5:2; 1 John 4:19-20

Day 7: Proof in the Pudding

What Does God Say?
If you love me, keep my commandments.
John 14:15

Have you ever met someone who verbally professed to be a Christian, but nothing about them aligned with their confession. Their lifestyle was extremely contrary to the life that a Christian should be living. The world likes to call these "Christians" hypocrites.

In scripture, Jesus would often refer to the Sadducees and Pharisees such a way. He would scold them for being the spiritual authorities of the Jews who knew the laws by heart yet did not obey the same laws they condemned others for breaking. Jesus often called them hypocrites and a viperous generation! They apparently worked his nerves! Not because they were sinners who had a repented heart, but because they were sinners who completely overlooked or ignored their own faults. They had no desire to change.

We all struggle. The Bible says that all have sinned and fallen short of the glory of God. However, we cannot use the grace of God as our green light to willfully disobey God. To willfully disobey God on a repeated basis should not be our ultimate goal. Our ultimate goal should be to overcome sin until we reach complete victory!

From the Inside Out

As believers, the closer we get to the Father through Christ and His Holy Spirit, the less we want to stay in a position of separation from Him. Sin drives a wedge between God and us. Although, nothing can separate us from His love, sin will keep us from growing in God and from getting closer to Him. Therefore, something indeed has to change.

If we consistently look no different from the world, the something that has to change is our souls. Soul in the Greek translation means mind, will, and imaginations (emotions). Our minds have to be changed, renewed, and transformed. Our will has to align with the Father's will. Everything about us has to change from the inside out!

When this change begins to occur, we want to do differently and to be different. We don't want to talk the same, walk the same, or go about life aimless, without purpose and without guidance. We want to obey God's commands: to love Him with everything that is us and to love our neighbors as we love our own selves. All of the laws and the Ten Commandments can be hinged on love! Why? Our love for God makes us want to do anything to please Him and to avoid everything that would hurt Him.

The Journey Begins...

Of course, this is a process. I would argue a life-long one. Nevertheless, when we take the first step towards God, He will grant us the strength, the grace, and the power to overcome every weight that may have once easily caused us to slip and slide.

The great news is that we are not alone! God is with us every step of the way, and He is faithful and just to complete what He began in us when we said yes to Him.

God is not finished with us yet! There is hope, and Christ has already overcome the world. The fight is fixed. We have victory over sin and over the death that will ensue because of it!

Dear Jesus,

Thank you for this journey! Thank you that as long as we walk with you and abide in You, You will keep our feet from slipping. We thank you, Lord, that You have given us victory over sin. Teach us your ways, and we will follow You. May our obedience to You demonstrate our absolute love for You!

In Your Name We Pray,
Amen

Food for the Spirit Dessert

1 John 5:2-3; 1 Peter 1:8; Ephesians 6:24; John 14:21-24

Work My Faith
Putting Love to the Test

As believers, we have the ability to look to the ultimate example of who love is and how love should be given by God Himself. From placing Jesus in reserve after the fall of Adam and Eve in the garden to Jesus undergoing the supreme sacrifice for mankind on the cross of Calvary, God has demonstrated with great strength and power *Love*. What is more, God, in all of His infinite wisdom, displays His love through the words and actions of the people we encounter each and every day. The following Work My Faith tools have been developed to help you put love into practice. You can try them all, or you can choose the activity that you feel best suits where you are and offers you what you need.

1. **Find My Freedom:** In life we all have experienced hurt and disappointments. If you haven't, live a little longer, and you will! Just like being born and dying, hurt and disappointment are universal. For a moment, let us consider those people who have not properly loved us. We first want to acknowledge that they may not have been able to offer you what they didn't have or know how to give. Perhaps a parent was not in the picture, or they were in the picture, but were not very affectionate. Consider how love was or was not shown to that parent. Was there a father or mother in the picture? Did they have to fend for themselves? Were they raised in a generation in which being the provider was synonymous with "showing" love? Did someone tell them they were loved on a regular basis?

   - Ever heard the saying, walk a mile in my shoes before you judge me? This exercise is designed to help you to see through rose tinted glasses. I want you to think about one to two people in your life who did not love you the way you felt you deserved to be loved. Now think about what they said, did, or did not do that made you feel unloved. In your journal, jot down at least five words to describe how their actions left you feeling. For example, if your father was absent from your life, you may have been left feeling rejected and abandoned.

- Next, record two to three things that you know about their life that you think may have contributed to who they are or how they were. Reflect on what you have written. Now write down three reasons why you should forgive him/her/them collectively for not giving you the love you desired or the love you needed.

- This will become our point of reference when we go before God in prayer. Everything on your paper, lift this up to God praying specifically for the power to forgive, the power to love, and the power to let go. Finally, tear this paper out of your journal and bury it: in the back yard, in a flower pot, in a garden, or wherever you may choose. This action will symbolize your releasing this hurt and disappointed to God and finally letting it go.

2. **What Does Love Look Like:** In your journal, I want you to draw a line down the center of the page. Near the top of your line, draw another line that will intersect it horizontally. Yes, you have guessed it, you are making a T chart. Do this on both sides of your paper.

- On the upper left side of your first T chart write: *Who Loves Me* and on the upper right side write: *How Do I Know.* Underneath your heading on the left try to list at least five people in your life who you know really love you.

- Now on the right, list what they say, do, or don't do that makes you feel loved. Try to list at least five details for each person. Now, flip this page over to your second T chart and write: *Who Hasn't Loved Me* on the upper left side of your chart. On the upper right side write: *How Do I Know?* Now, on the left underneath your heading list two to three people in your life who you feel should have loved you but didn't or couldn't. Now on the right, list what each person said, didn't say, did or didn't do that affirmed that what they were displaying was not love. This may be more difficult than the first list, but I want you to be both open and honest.

- On a separate sheet of paper or, if you prefer, in the space left over underneath one of your T charts, record what this exercise revealed to you about what love does and does not look like. Did you notice any trends good or bad? How did it make you feel when you were listing the attributes or the actions of the people who you know truly love you? How did you feel listing the names and the behavior or attributes of the people who you feel did not love you?

- Now that we have a clear picture of what love does and does not look like, this, again, will be the focus to our prayers. This morning or tonight, whatever your specified prayer time will be, pray that God will help you to love like you have been loved. Be specific. Be open. Be transparent. This gives God room to started tilling the soil of your heart so that His love can begin to grow and flourish in every area of your life.

3. **Putting Love Into Action:** This week we have been introduced to Love, Himself, God Almighty. We have studied and meditated on what God has to say about love. Now it's time to start applying this love in our lives. The people in your life who have shown you love did so out of a selfless loyalty to you. You may not have always been loving or lovable in return, but they loved you anyway. What can you model from your loved ones? How do you currently show love to people you know *and* to strangers? In the upcoming weeks, I want you to be very purposeful to be more selfless, patient, and kind. Trust me, this will not be easy. And you will be presented with countless opportunities to make the choice to love instead of making the choice to be selfish, impatient, and not so nice. Remember we are on a journey. This means, learning to love; and choosing to love is a process, so be encouraged! If you fall short in one moment, strive to hit the nail on the head in the next.

4. **Speak Life to Breathe Life:** So far this week, we have been given some delectable Food for the Spirit Dessert to continue to chew over in our spare time. For this exercise, choose any two of those scriptures, and write each one on a Post-it note. Post your scriptures in two places that you are guaranteed to see as you go about your daily lives. Perhaps the bathroom mirror or on the back of the front door would be ideal places to post them. These verses will become our scriptural affirmations designed to motivate us to continue

loving even when it is not so easy to do. Eventually, these scriptures will become committed to memory and our inspirational mantras.

Week 2: **Joy**

What is joy? This is a question that, I believe, puzzles many people. Joy is often mistaken to be synonymous with happiness. In fact, the dictionary defines joy as a feeling of great pleasure or happiness.

In the Bible, the English word joy is used several times to translate many different Hebrew words. For example, the Hebrew word *gihl* means a revolution of time, but is translated as joy in the Bible. Another Hebrew word for joy would be *masows* meaning an object of joy, delight, or mirth. The Hebrew word *samach* means to brighten up or to be gleesome. Additionally, the Greek translation for joy is *chara* meaning joy or delight.

Now with all this information, we are still left asking, "What is joy, and how do I get some?" Have you ever heard that old gospel song that says, "This joy that I have, the world didn't give it to me, and the world can't take it away!" When defining joy, I would like to start right there. Joy is not something that this world or the things in this world can give to you nor can it take away from you.

You see, happiness is based on what's happening in our lives or in our world. If you haven't noticed, the world is ever-evolving and the events of our lives change dramatically from day to day and sometimes from one moment to the next. Therefore, if joy was based on what's happening, it would be subject to fluctuate. It would be vulnerable to our feelings and by what is happening to us or around us.

Similar to love, joy is, thankfully, not contingent on our external environment. Happiness is. When all is well—finances, marriage, kids, health, career, the economy, or the national defense—naturally, we are happy. Why not? Everything is perfect. Right?

But what about when all isn't well in our world? A recession hits, your health fails, your marriage is on the rocks, your children have lost their minds, there is drama at the work place, you are laid off, or you fall into debt. Simply put, life happens, and happiness will not be anywhere to be found. Happiness will be powerless to sustain you, but joy won't! be

This week, we are going to focus our faith and our energy on developing joy in our hearts and in our lives. Indeed, the questions of "What is joy?" and "How do I get it" will be answered in this week's devotionals, and we will, by faith, begin experiencing the joy of the Lord like never before!

Day 8: Unspeakable Joy

What Does God Say?

May the God of hope fill you with all joy and peace as you trust in him, so that you may overflow with hope by the power of the Holy Spirit.
Romans 15:13

Two years ago I was in the scariest place of my adult life. I was nine months pregnant and was released from my job a week before I was expected to give birth. No job meant no health insurance on top of all of our other financial responsibilities that were certain to compound without a steady income coming in to pay them. If you are not aware, delivering a baby in a hospital is astronomically expensive, and to have to pay for it out of pocket would be preposterous. Needless to say, my husband and I were petrified.

My former employer offered me a severance package that would allow my health insurance to be extended for one more month. They also offered to pay me two more checks. I reluctantly accepted the package because I was desperate! I felt that my options were slim and that I simply did not have any other choice but to accept what was on the table.

The Bottom Fell Out

This decision bought us some time: a few weeks at best. My husband was self-employed, so the income that came from him was not always consistent, which was to be expected building a new business. Nevertheless, the bills were due, and then they were past due, and, well, you can guess the rest. Between my husband and my unemployment income, we managed to keep our eyelids above water!

I remember being so angry and afraid. I was angry at God. I was angry at my employer. My fear of God had heightened in a non-reverential way. I could not understand why God would allow this to happen. We already had a two year old daughter and, now, a newborn baby that we really could not afford at this point.

We had done everything right. We were married. We both were employed. We both had multiple degrees. We waited to have children when we were able to afford them, but that security in ourselves and our abilities was now completely stripped directly from underneath us.

Do You Believe It?

Months went by, and I was unable to find employment. My husband and I were sinking deeper into debt. Our home was now in danger of being foreclosed upon. Unsurprisingly, I was spiraling deeper into depression, and I felt so helpless. I was so frustrated. My confidence in God was shaken. Or so I thought…

I remember sitting in the kitchen of my friend's home. I was sharing with her my feelings about everything. My voice was shaky with panic and dripping with bitterness. However, she was unmoved.

My friend simply looked at me and said, "Well, you don't trust God…" I was rattled with offense.

"I trust God!" was my swift rebuttal.

"Well, you don't know His word."

Now even more offended, I retorted, "I know His word!"

"Well, do you believe it?"

I wanted to fire something back in my own defense, but I was stunned. She had called my bluff, and she had challenged me to put my faith where my mouth was! It was at that moment that I realized that I really *didn't* trust God nor did I truly *believe* His word. That is where my journey to Jesus truly began.

All Things Are Working Together

Looking back, I am so thankful for that time. My husband and I grew closer. I was able to spend invaluable time with my daughters that my previous job did not allow me the liberty to do. And, above everything else, God taught me to trust in Him and not in my employer or in myself. I learned that God was my provider, and I am telling you, the favor and grace that He poured out on our behalf was nothing short of miraculous.

This trying experience began to produce a quiet confidence in the God I serve. Joy, unspeakable joy, swells in my heart now because I understand that **all** things work together for my good because I love God and because God loves me.

Trials perfect us. They make us better, and they give God the opportunity to show off on our behalf. I trust God now like never before, and I speak His word over every situation that I face. I speak it until it becomes more real and more tangible than what my eyes can see and what my emotions can feel. It is through the power of His most Holy Spirit that I am filled with joy because I am learning to trust in Him no matter what! Let your trust in God release this same joy in your life in a mighty way!

Dear Jesus,

You are so very faithful! We thank You that everything we need we can find it in You! Teach us to trust You above our own ability, the economy, or anything that may come to shake our faith. Thank you God for the joy that is found in trusting You. Fill us with this joy until we are overflowing with the hope that what you promised will come to pass.

In Your Name We Pray,
Amen

Food for the Spirit Dessert
Romans 12:12; 2 Corinthians 9:8; Romans 14:17

Day 9: There's Purpose

What Does God Say?

...fixing our eyes on Jesus, the pioneer and perfecter of faith. For the joy set before him he endured the cross, scorning its shame, and sat down at the right hand of the throne of God.
Hebrews 12:2

Have you ever found yourself on the other side of a problem only to look back and understand why you endured what you'd endured? I know that I have had my share of "aha moments" where it was suddenly crystal clear as to how my "problem" had worked out for my ultimate benefit.

Thankfully, over the course of my life I can see how the same unfortunate, painful, frustrating circumstances had in the long run protected me, directed me, and corrected me when it was all said and done. I came out of it all stronger, wiser, and better than before...There was a purpose for the pain.

In the Midst of It

Now, while we are in the midst of our problems, it is not so easy to be optimistic. In fact, sometimes it is downright difficult to see the rainbow beyond life's storms. Why? Because pain hurts! But I am so grateful that we serve a God, who loves us in return! There are some things that God allows us to endure to make us better than our former selves; to get something important to us; or to accomplish something powerful through us...There is a purpose for the pain.

Christ so graciously endured the cross. He endured the shame, the scorn, the PAIN, the humiliation, and the degradation because there is purpose even when there is pain! Christ understood and caused Himself to focus on the Big Picture even as He endured the cross.

Surely, He could have called legions of angels to come down and war on His behalf, but He understood His purpose. He was intimate with the truth that the cross and that His enduring the cross, would save a dying world and restore man unto God Himself. He comprehended that what He was to suffer for that moment in time, would forever alter eternity. So He willingly endured the cross for the joy that was to come!

All Working for Good

Kind of like a mother nine months pregnant and *ready* to give birth, she must endure the agony of labor, but she does so for the joy set before her, holding her bundle of joy in her arms when the labor pains are finished and the delivery is accomplished.

EVERYTHING we will ever face in our walks with Christ is a part of a plan so much greater than ourselves. As Romans 8:28 remind us, "All things work together for the good to them that love the Lord and are called according to His purpose." Beloved, nothing that you have ever endured or will ever endure is in vain. God is the expert in turning our mess into a message, our tests into testimonies, and our pain into something to sing about! Indeed, we have joy set before us!

Dear Jesus,

Thank you for always being here with us. Thank you that no matter what we face, we are never alone. Lord, teach us to see the Big Picture so that we can rejoice in you come rain or shine!

In Your Name We Pray,
Amen

Food for the Spirit Dessert

1 Corinthians 9:24-27; 2 Timothy 4:7; Hebrews 12:1

Day 10: I Want More

What Does God Say?

The kingdom of heaven is like treasure hidden in a field. When a man found it, he hid it again, and then in his joy went and sold all he had and bought that field.
Matthew 13:44

The deeper you delve into God's word, the closer you get to Christ. The more diligently you work God's word in your life, the more you will begin to enter into the joy of the Lord! I've already shared with you how my life as a Christian became very haphazard. I was on top one day and down in the muck and mire the next. I had been outwardly going through the motions of Christianity: obligatory praying, attending church, paying my tithes, and serving perfunctorily in church ministries.

I recall going to church, hearing a good word and leaving church excited and, simply, feeling good; but then, sometimes before I even left the parking lot, something trivial would occur, and those warm, fuzzy feelings would dissipate.

You see, I had the ritual of Christianity down packed. Nonetheless, I was void of having a true relationship with Christ. I had to eventually admit that I had years under my belt, but that even in all of that time, my understanding of God and His word was shallow.

All I Need Is You, Lord!

I had no joy, no peace, and the love of Christ was not overflowing in my heart and spilling out into my life. I mean, I loved God and I wanted to please Him, but I was not seeing His Word made manifest in my life, consistently. Eventually, I got tired of experiencing overwhelming defeat in my walk with Christ, and I decided that I wanted more of Him, and I wasn't going to stop until I got it!

When I made the decision to really seek God, life began, and almost immediately, I was introduced to joy! God the Father, through His Son, Jesus Christ, and by way of His marvelous Holy Spirit has to become more precious to us than the rarest jewel or the most magnificent masterpiece! God has to be more coveted to us than all of the money, fame, and riches that this world can offer... When we arrive at the place of *All I Need Is You*, Lord, we will desire to please God. We will long to bring Him glory. We will yearn to spend as much time with Him as earthly possible because He becomes everything.

This awakening allows for joy to be developed within us. It is in this place that joy begins to manifest itself in our hearts. Ultimately, joy will manifest a submitted life and a committed heart in which our sole purpose is to live for, to love, and to be the delight of Christ.

Dear Jesus,

We thank you that there are no limitations to how close we can get to you. We thank you that there is always more to learn about you, more to understand about your Word, and more to love about you. Thank you for desiring a friendship with us. May our hearts always long for your presence and for your fellowship. You are our joy!

In Your Name We Pray,
Amen

Food for the Spirit Dessert
Matthew 6:21; Proverbs 2:2-5; John 6:35

Day 11: God Bless the Faithful

What Does God Say?

Those who sow with tears will reap with songs of joy.

Psalm 126:5

There is something about being faithful…For years and years you do what's right regardless of who sees you, regardless of who says thank you, or regardless of what it costs you. I remember as a child watching my mother serve. Mama had a servant's heart. She took care of everyone around her.

If she could cook you a meal and feed you until you were stuffed, she would. She would give you a place to stay to help you get back on your feet; she would gladly open her doors. If you needed a few dollars to tide you over until the next check, she would give it without hesitation…She was consistent in putting the needs of others and the well-being of someone else over her own. This was her nature. It was indeed how God made her.

Got Till It's Gone

Consequently, Mama gave so much that some of the people around her became glorified leeches. They often would suck her dry on a regular basis, but this didn't stop her from being who she was created to be: a nurturer. This bounce-back Spirit that she seemed to possess, however, was not exempt from experiencing pain and disappointment.

I cannot count the amount of times I witnessed my mom crying over the hurt that someone she'd helped had caused. I watched how she would prepare food for others to enjoy for them to not leave her anything to eat when it was all said and done. I watched her work her fingers to the bone to care for my siblings, her siblings and her mother, often with no assistance from anyone. Yet, the one thing I remember the most about my mama was that she always had a warm smile on her face, a boisterous laugh that was contagious upon hearing, and a gentle heart that never seemed to run out of love and forgiveness.

You Reap What You Sow

You see, I didn't understand it then, but Mama had an understanding about love, God, and life that I lacked in my adolescence. She didn't look for man to reward her, to celebrate her, or to honor her; yet, her generous heart gave her favor with so many that she was often rewarded, celebrated, and honored for who she was. She sowed countless tears, but God allowed her to reap a joy that cannot be understood. He rewarded her with joy for all of the pain that she'd endured. She loved her family, her friends, and her life, and she was truly loved by so many in return.

Mama is no longer with us in the natural. She passed away thirteen years ago. I will never forget her funeral service. The spacious Catholic church that we had been raised in was filled beyond capacity with the people whose lives had been richly impacted by the joy within my mother! She touched each and every one of the people seated and standing, lining the walls all around the sanctuary, all there to pay their respect to this little woman with a gigantic heart.

Dear Jesus,

Lord, we thank you that as we are faithful to you and your word, you will honor our faithfulness. Teach us to see you in every trial that we face, and teach us to travel gracefully through life's storms with peace, joy, and faith.

In Your Name We Pray,
Amen

Food for the Spirit Dessert
Matthew 5:4; Isaiah 35:10; Galatians 6:9

Day 12: It's Morning!

What Does God Say?

Weeping may last through the night, but joy comes with the morning.
Psalm 30:5b

The longer I live, the more I have come to learn that life happens to us all. Whether rich or poor, we all will have trials and tribulations to face at some point. Losing a loved one, seasons of financial woe, job loss, marital conflict, sickness, wayward children, car problems, family issues, or problems on the job...life will indeed happen to us all.

It is in these moments that we understandably want to throw a pity party: *'Woe is me and everything around me'*. We want to scream, shout, cry, hide, and run; we want to pass the blame... Simply put, we're hurting and angry, and we want this new found trouble to pass just as swiftly as it came.

In the blink of an eye, our pristine worlds can be turned upside down, right side up, and upside down once again! That's life. It can be unpredictable. We all have a season of weeping, but the key is to embrace it as such: just...a...season.

The Same 24 Hours

When we think about the twenty-four hours of each day that God grants to every man, we know that nighttime does not last forever. No matter how dark that night may seem. No matter how stormy that night may get, it *will* end; morning *will* come each and every day.

We can accept the same reality for our lives. Weeping may endure for the night, but joy comes in the morning. Why? Morning brings hope, it brings new opportunities, and it brings new possibilities.

I know it doesn't always feel like it. I know it hurts more than you could ever imagine. I know you are afraid, confused, and frustrated, but joy comes in the morning. I know it looks bleak…I know it is the darkest that you have ever seen it, but joy comes in the morning.

He Is a Promise Keeper

Notice the scripture does not give the conditional helping verb "will" before comes. This, I believe, is because this scripture is one of the many promises that God has given to us as His sons and daughters. This is a verse that is certain to come to pass for you in your due season. So hold on through your night experience. Don't lose your faith, and don't lose heart. Your morning is coming! Rejoice!

Dear Jesus,
We thank you that you are not a man that you should lie. We are grateful that you are faithful to accomplish what you've promised; it will come to pass. Lord, as we face our nighttime experience, we thank you for never leaving our side; and we praise you for our joy and for our morning!

In Your Name We Pray,
Amen

Food for the Spirit Dessert
Psalm 6:6-9; Psalm 46:4-5; Hosea 6:3

Day 13: Oh, the Presence of the Lord

What Does God Say?

You make known to me the path of life; you will fill me with joy in your presence, with eternal pleasures at your right hand.

Psalm 16:11

There is nothing like the presence of the Lord! I remember when I first gave my life to Christ. I had never felt the presence of God before that moment, or if I had, I didn't recognize it. I felt as if the coziest, securest blanket had just enveloped me completely. I felt peace, a peace I had never felt before. God's presence just simply felt like home, and it was a home that I NEVER wanted to leave or be without again.

That was twelve years ago. Throughout the years, I have felt the presence of the Lord. I could not count the amount of times, but each time was just as precious, just as beautiful, and just as sacred as the very first experience.

Consider you're in a powerful worship service. Praise is high, and the pastor brings forth a word that speaks directly to what you're going through. Your hands are raised; tears are streaming down your face, and all you feel is peace. The load you entered into the sanctuary carrying has been lifted. The illness you arrived with has been healed. The depression or the oppression that had you bound has dissipated, and the only thing left in its stead is joy and a sweet peace. All of this is a result of the powerful presence of God.

Heart translates to *kardia* in the Greek which means the effective center of our being. More specifically, the heart of man is his center. It is in this center where one will find the mind, will, intentions, character, and emotions of that man. What makes this man who he is can be traced back to the contents of his heart.

Our Number One

When we make God our priority…when we desire nothing more than His perfect will and His presence for our lives, something miraculous happens! The God of the heavens and the earth comes and takes up residence within our hearts and makes the heart his dwelling place. And guess what happens? His will becomes our will. God's character and intentions becomes our character and intentions. His thoughts become our thoughts, and on and on it goes.

What does this have to do with joy? Everything! When we understand that God has a perfect plan for our lives, we can have joy about tomorrow. When we catch the revelation that God is in our tomorrow, we have joy about today. And, when we acknowledge God, praise God, thank God, and honor God in everything that we do, we experience the powerful presence of God every day of our lives. This revelation that the Creator of the universe wants to dwell within us, walk with us, and talk with us every day of our lives brings beautiful, unspeakable joy!

Dear Jesus,

Fill us with the joy that abides in your beautiful, magnificent presence. Thank you for your presence. Thank you for your sweet Holy Spirit. Lord, give us a heart like yours. May we desire you above all else.

In Your Name We Pray,
Amen

Food for the Spirit Dessert

Jude 1:24; 2 Corinthians 4:17; Isaiah 2:3

Day 14: You Win!

What Does God Say?
The LORD your God is with you, the Mighty Warrior who saves.
He will take great joy in you; in his love he will no longer rebuke you, but will rejoice
over you with singing.
Zephaniah 3:17

W e live in a time of uncertainty. Unemployment is on the rise. Gas and grocery prices are exorbitant. There are violent uprises globally. Every week it seems there is yet another broadcast about a mass shooting in a school, in a church, in a mall, or in some other very public establishment. The weather has been erratic. Unrest...Discord...Lawlessness...Rebellion...and all appears to be a sign of the times.

It is this uncertainty that places fear in the hearts of many. So many are worried how they are going to feed their families. They wonder how they are going to rebound after catastrophe. Things seem bleak, and so many are losing hope in the systems that continue to keep failing all around them.

Allow me to encourage you. No matter what the government does or does not do. No matter which direction the wind may blow... God is with you! You are not alone! He is not oblivious to the world around you.

He Is Mighty to Save

God is Mighty to Save! He can and will rescue you out of ALL of your troubles, so just trust Him. Trust Him and not your circumstances.

Dare to believe His word and not what you see in this world. As believers, we don't have to fear the darkness of this world. We are the children of the only living God who is MIGHTY to save, mighty to heal, and mighty to deliver us from every recession, calamity, and natural disaster that may come to steal, kill, and destroy!

Know that God is warring on your behalf! He has not forgotten, so hold fast to your promises! All of them. Don't know what God has promised you? He's given you sixty-six books filled with promises just for you also known as the Holy Bible. Keep praying. Keep fasting. Keep believing. Keep walking upright, and all you will have to do is stand still and see the salvation of the Lord! He will indeed rejoice over you, His child, with singing! He has given you the victory over sickness, over poverty, over broken relationships, over addiction, over depression, over anxiety, and over sin! Hear me when I say, You WIN!

Dear Jesus,

Hallelujah to your name! You are awesome, and you are mighty! Lord, we thank you that you have not given us a spirit of fear, but one of love, power, and a sound mind. We thank you that we can place our trust in you with confidence knowing that you are with us! Thank you for being our Savior! Thank you Lord that you are fighting on our behalves and that you have given us the victory!

In Your Name We Pray,
Amen

Food for the Spirit Dessert
Acts 2:28; Jude 1:24-25; Psalm 21:4-6

Work My Faith
Got Joy?

God desires for us to have hearts filled with joy. He desires for us to have a joy within that is not shaken by the uncertainty without. Remember, joy is a quiet confidence that God is with you, wherever you are. No matter what we face, everything is working together for our good. However, far too many believers do not have joy. They experience fleeting moments of happiness, but not the sustaining power of joy. This week's Work My Faith tools will be completely dedicated to helping you cultivate the joy that you have rightly inherited when you accepted Christ as your personal Lord and Savior! Again, you can try them all, or you can choose the activity that you feel ministers to where you are.

1. **The Presence of the Lord**: Apart from God, I would boldly argue that Joy does not exist! So, logically, if we want joy, then we need God. This assignment will help you to purposely dedicate time with our beautiful Savior so that you may begin to be filled with joy. The ultimate goal is to gradually dedicate a few more minutes as your quiet time with God continues.

   - Starting today I want you to set aside at least ten minutes of "God and Me Time". For ten to fifteen minutes, no cell phone. No computer. No television; not even your family. Unplug and get away to a secluded area that is peaceful to you. This area could be your bedroom, your bathroom, your car, a park, or wherever you can relax and focus on God.

   - Once you've unplugged and you've found a relaxing place, take a few deep breaths to clear your mind from the activities of the day.

- Next, begin to simply reflect over your day. Consider the good and the not so good. Now begin to verbally thank God for what you are thankful for today. You can be thankful for anything: beautiful weather, safe travel to and from work, a parking space near the front entrance of a store, your children, the use of your limbs, etc. You'll find that thanksgiving and gratitude tend to lighten your mood and help to change your perspective.

- Now that your heart is filled with thanksgiving, tell God about what is in your heart. Your fears, your concerns, your desires, your struggles, your requests. Bring it all before the Lord in prayer with the intentions to leave it with Him.

- Take time to thank God again, praising Him in advance for answering your prayers!

- Alright, now in your last few minutes of alone time with God, I want you to simply silence your thoughts and quiet your soul. **Now, listen**...God desires to speak to us all of the time, but very seldomly do we make the time to listen. I would also use this time of **listening** to read the word. The Bible is filled with the heartbeat of Jesus, His word, so the surest way to hear God's voice is by reading His word.

- As you continue to make time for God, the more frequently you will be able to experience his sweet presence, and in His presence, there *is* fullness of joy!

2. **A Purpose Driven Life:** Every man and woman on this earth was born with a purpose. Jeremiah 29:11 shares with us that God has good thoughts toward us; He has a plan for us to succeed and not to fail. When we accept Christ, we accept God's perfect plan for our lives; and it is God's desire that we fulfill the destiny that He has for

each and every one of us. For one reason or another we do not pursue our passions or go after what it is we really want out of life. This exercise will help you to get the ball rolling towards being who you were created to be. Understanding why you are on this planet and beginning to fulfill your purpose, will produce a joy deep within.

- In your journals make a list of all of the things that you love to do. This list should include all of the things that you could do all day every day for the rest of your life and not be paid a dime for doing. Be specific. For example, I love to help people in whatever capacity I'm needed in. I would add my love to help people to my list.

- Now I want you to make another list. This list will include all of the things that irritate you the most about society, about the government, about the school system, about whatever. What problem gets underneath your skin? For instance, it irritates me beyond measure to come across students who are teenagers that are reading significantly below grade level. This irritates me because I feel as if the school system has failed this child.

- Next, look over the first list you've made. Now ask yourself, 'Of all the things that I love to do, what am I currently doing in my life that gives me the opportunity to do what I love on a consistent basis?' If you cannot think of one single way in which you are able to engage in this passion, it is time to get to work. The next exercise will be specifically for you. However, if you can see where you engage in this passion, list all of the ways in which you can spend more time or devote more energy into doing what you love.

- Finally, review the second list. Consider what problem irritates you. Now consider what you can possibly do to help solve this problem, if not completely than partially? Using my example again, if it irritates me to see teens reading below grade level, then it is part of my life's mission to help the teens that come through my classroom to begin reading at or above grade level by the time they leave me. This may require some creativity and some dedication on my part to strive to accomplish this. I may even miss the mark at times, but as long as I am working to resolve this problem or this irritant, I am fulfilling my life's purpose, and joy is steadily welling up within!

3. **A Step in the Right Direction:** If you cannot think of one single way in which you are able to engage in your passion, this exercise is specifically for you. Make another list. This time I want you to list all of the careers and/ or volunteer opportunities that would allow you to utilize your gifts or talents on a consistent basis. For instance, if you like to help people get well, perhaps you would want to find a career or volunteer in the medical field. If you love to cook, you could prepare meals and share them with people in your community or with a local homeless shelter. If you love computers, maybe you want to go to school and be trained formally to design websites and programs. You could also volunteer your skill to local businesses that could use your technological expertise to take their business to the next level, but they cannot yet afford the service. After you have made this list, select one career opportunity or volunteer opportunity that you would be willing to try out. Now, take one step towards this opportunity today. This could mean, performing an internet search for careers, schools/programs, or volunteer opportunities that will allow you to start doing what you love. Prayerfully, this step will lead to the next step of applying, enrolling, or volunteering as soon as possible!

4. **Speak Life to Breathe Life:** For this exercise, again, choose any three of the scriptures from this week's Food for the Spirit Desserts, and write each one on a Post-it note. This time post your scriptures in three places that you are guaranteed to see them as you go about your daily routine. These verses will be this week's scriptural affirmations designed to motivate you to continue to incubate joy within your soul. Again, eventually these scriptures will become committed to memory where they will work as your inspirational mantras!

Week 3: **Peace**

Peace is something that many want but few truly have. It is difficult to turn on the television without seeing a commercial advertising the latest pharmaceutical "answer" to anxiety and depression. The state of the economy and the political unrest in this country alone keeps many people stressed out and nervous.

People pay hundreds and sometimes thousands of dollars on self-help books, seminars, conferences and the like in hopes to buy some peace. Others pay the psychiatrist and the psychologist to help them understand why they have no peace and to help them make the depression, stress, and pain go away with an activity or a pill. Sex, drugs, alcohol, money, partying, you name it, many are willing to indulge in it if it means gaining just a little peace, even if for a moment. The Universe, energy, a higher power, Buddha, Muhammad, eastern philosophy, science, and self have all been sought after to find peace or to earn a ticket to an eternal peace.

Regardless of the means to get there, we all want peace. No matter who you are, how much money you do or do not have, or what race you are, we **all** just want peace.

As Christians, we have the Spirit of the most High God living within us! This is the same Spirit that raised Jesus from the dead and gave Him the power to perform every miracle recorded in the Bible. So how is it that so many of us have all of this power on the inside of us, but we are not manifesting this attribute of Christ in our lives?

The Hebrew word for peace is *shalom*. Shalom can be translated to mean contentment, wholeness, completeness, and well-being and harmony. Without peace, we cannot function at our full potential. We are not able to live life abundantly. We are literally in bondage to worry, stress, depression, and the like until we find peace; and sustaining peace—peace that does not come with side effects or empty promises—only comes from

Christ! Jesus is the Prince of Peace, and as co-heirs with Christ, we have inherited peace. In this final week of our journey for spiritual growth, we want to focus on cultivating the fruit of the spirit *peace* within our everyday lives.

Day 15: Let Peace Have Her Way

What Does God Say?

Let the peace of Christ rule in your hearts, since as members of one body
you were called to peace. And be thankful.
Colossians 3:15

In this verse, the Apostle Paul is speaking to the church of Colossae. He implores the church to be united by love in the previous verse. Specifically, he instructs them to love each other and to forgive each other before we arrive at the above verse where he now tells the church to let the peace of Christ rule in their hearts as members of one body.

I have been in church all of my life, and as an adult it is even more prevalent that Sunday morning, and for some, Saturday morning is the most segregated day of the week. People work together, they live in the same neighborhoods, and participate in various social and recreational activities together; however, they don't seem to worship together.

Members of One Body

Now, I am certain there was some sort of discord amongst the members in the congregation of Colassae, and this letter was to restore peace. Nevertheless, I think that we can look at this scripture from a broader perspective. Sunday morning segregation has been very effective at keeping the body of Christ divided. Different denominations, varied doctrine, musical genre, dress code, and the like have created a disunity and discord that has hindered our effectiveness in the earth.

If I think I am right, then, naturally, I will think you are wrong and vice- verse. This dissension creates a dislike and, in some cases, a disdain from one church to the other. If I think you are wrong, then we spend unnecessary time arguing, debating, and tearing each other down. Ultimately, when this occurs, we have no peace in the church. And if the church lacks peace, then we are not acting as members of the same body— the body of Christ.

It should be our desire to please Christ, and it pleases Christ for us to be *one* even as He and the Father are one. We are the light of the world; we are a city on a hill, or we should be. The Bible says that we will be known by the love we have for one another. If a nonbeliever sees the disunity and the dissension amongst Christians, what will entice them to become one of us?

We need peace within the body of Christ now more than ever. The world is growing colder and darker by the moment. People are more rebellious and lawless now than, I'd argue, they've ever been. Many are lost and oblivious to the state of their souls. They need to see us as the ultimate example of what salvation, liberty, and life look like.

As individual believers and local churches, we can accomplish only so much. But together united as believers across the borders of denominations, doctrine, race, and class, we can take cities, counties, states, regions, and nations and point them to the Savior of the World, King Jesus! Let there be peace amongst us, and let that peace rule in our hearts always!

Dear Jesus,

We pray that our hearts would change towards one other and that we would be knit together in love and forgiveness. Allow the world to desire You as they see the peace we walk in together as one body and as one family.

In Your Name We Pray,
Amen

Food for the Spirit Dessert

John 14:27; Ephesians 2:14-16; Colossians 3:17

Day 16: Don't Let Go

What Does God Say?

They must turn from evil and do good; they must seek
peace and pursue it.
1 Peter 3:11

This is one of my favorite scriptures. I am reminded of it whenever I find myself in a situation that screams for peace. It is in those moments that I have to take inventory of my life. You see, sometimes we don't have peace within or our peace within is disturbed because of an outside stimulant. That stimulant can vary from moment to moment or from person to person. For instance, the stimulant could be a neighbor, a co-worker, a significant other; or it could be our health, our finances, and on it goes. Whatever the stimulant or stimulants are they are what I like to call Peace Robbers.

Their sole purpose, it seems in that moment, is to come and steal your peace. You've had a long day at work and you come home expecting to relax, unwind, and dwell in a peaceful atmosphere, and what happens? Your children or your spouse start acting crazy! Or your boss seems to be singling you out on a regular basis to share with you how everything you do is not good enough when you know you are giving it your 110%. How about the disgruntled customer or store clerk? What about that person who cuts you off in traffic or the neighbor who keeps throwing trash in your yard? Whatever the scenario is, if we are not careful, the minutest things can come and successfully rob us of our peace.

Guard You Hearts

As a result, we have to guard our hearts and not allow any old thing to come in and steal what does not belong to it. Although what you can face on a daily basis might be stressful or daunting, you can still maintain peace. This should be our goal.

How do we accomplish this? By seeking peace, and once we find it, not letting it go! When we seek God, daily drawing closer to Him in prayer and by His word, we are seeking peace; and when we find the peace of God, no one has the right or the power to take it away.

This means that someone or something can only have our peace when we give it to them. Perhaps you have to walk away from certain situations, or perhaps you have to hold your tongue. In some cases, you may have to leave some people behind. Whatever the case me be, hold on to your peace and continue to position yourself to have peace and to dwell in that peace consistently.

Dear Jesus,

We seek you. We seek your heart. Give us wisdom and guide us in the process of seeking peace and pursuing it! We thank you that peace is readily available to us as believers. Again, we receive our peace, and we chose to preserve it for your glory!

In Your Name We Pray,
Amen

Food for the Spirit Dessert
Psalm 34:14; Matthew 5:9; Romans 12:18

Day 17: It Belongs to You

What Does God Say?

For to us a child is born, to us a son is given, and the government will be on his shoulders. And he will be called Wonderful Counselor, Mighty God, Everlasting Father, Prince of Peace.
Isaiah 9:6

When God the Father gifted Christ to this earth, He in turn gifted to the world peace. As Christians, we have a right to peace. This means that we don't have to go without peace another moment! Just like joy, peace is another aspect of the fruit of the Spirit that many Christians are lacking. We know the scriptures, or maybe we do. We can attend church faithfully. We may have accepted Christ as our personal Lord and savior, but some of us still don't have peace. Why?

Why is it that so many believers lack peace or, at least, lack a consistent peace? I believe the answer lies in the reality that some do not believe that it is possible. Given the myriad of trials that we all face in this life, maintaining a consistent peace within ourselves or within our individual worlds seem unattainable; this idea to many is foreign.

However, peace *can* rule in our hearts. We can and should have peace within and peace around us regardless of the trials we face or the circumstances that we endure because God has given us the Prince of Peace, Jesus.

Go Get Your Inheritance!

His Holy Spirit lives within each of us, so Holy Spirit is our key to peace. When Christ ascended into Heaven to be seated at the right hand of the Father, in His place He sent us the comforter, His Holy Spirit. Jesus did not leave without sending back a piece of Himself to help us through this journey called life.

Holy Spirit is the power of God in this earth, and He is our peace. Simply put, we have the Spirit of the living God living, breathing, and working on the inside of us. Whatever we may face, we have access to an everlasting peace within us.

By the grace of God, we have the ability to have peace seven days a week, 24 hours a day. We have the privilege to have peace in our hearts, in our minds, in our homes, and on our jobs because God came to this earth and because he left us a comforter.

You have inherited peace as joint heirs with Christ. So become determined to not go another moment without it! Go get your inheritance!

Dear Jesus,

Lord we ask for peace. Peace in our hearts, peace in our homes, and peace in our lives. God we willingly by faith receive your peace today! Thank you for hearing our prayers and for answering them faithfully!

In Your Name We Pray,
Amen

Food for the Spirit Dessert

Ephesians 2:14; Isaiah 11:1-2; Jeremiah 23:5-6

Day 18: Peace of Mind

What Does God Say?
You will keep in perfect peace those whose minds are steadfast, because they trust in you.
Isaiah 26:3

If there is anywhere that we need peace, it is in our minds. The mind is powerful. The Bible tells us that as a man thinks, so is he. How you see yourself is directly related to your thoughts about you. Consequently, the peace that we should desire is an internal peace or rest. This type of peace allows you to be steadfast, immovable, and unshakeable even in the greatest, most ferocious storms that life can bring. Surely, if you have peace within—peace in your mind—then you can weather anything, to include the catastrophic storm!

The fact of the matter is if you are shaken within your mind, then you have only been *temporarily* defeated because we have victory in Christ! So we have to work extra hard to keep our minds stayed on God. We can do this by knowing what the word says about that situation or circumstance, and once we know what God says about that thing through His word, we make an unprecedented choice. What do we choose? We choose to believe the word of the Lord over all else. We choose to uproot our "stinking thinking" and replace it with what God says. In other words, we, again, exchange the lie for the **truth**.

Choose to Believe

The doctor's report says doom and gloom, but God's word says that by His stripes we are healed, so choose to believe God's word over that of the doctor's report. Focus your mind on that word and every other scripture you can find in the Bible related to your healing, and meditate on that word(s) both day and night, and there will be peace within. Changing your thoughts will then empower you to eat fresh natural foods, for instance, and to become physically active, producing healing and creating peace!

Your marriage is failing miserably. Divorce court seems to be inevitable, but God's word says that what God has joined together let no man separate and that there is nothing too hard for our God. So you focus and meditate on these scriptures and fight for your marriage, and there will be peace in your mind; and soon, there will be peace in your marriage. Why? Your thoughts changed, hope was produced, and you chose to commit to work to create the marriage that you wanted.

When we trust God, when we trust His word, He promises to keep us in perfect peace because we have made the conscious effort to focus on Him; we've made the express decision to trust Him above all else. When we truly come to trust God, He will keep us from losing our minds; He will keep us from losing what is most dear to us, and He will bless us with perfect peace!

Dear Jesus,

We choose to trust you above all else. Help us to focus on you, the Problem Solver, and not on the problem. Thank you Lord for promising to keep us in perfect peace when we make the decision to trust you!

In Your Name We Pray,
Amen

Food for the Spirit Dessert
John 16:33; Jeremiah 17:7-8; Romans 4: 18-21

Day 19: Doesn't Make Any Sense

What Does God Say?

Be anxious for nothing, but in everything by prayer and supplication with thanksgiving let your requests be made known to God. And the peace of God, which surpasses all comprehension, will guard your hearts and your minds in Christ Jesus.
Philippians 4:7

W hen we pray, we have to believe that God has heard us and that He is answering our prayers in our due season. I am learning that the most challenging obstacle that comes to hinder our faith after we have prayed to God is time. Time is something that most people feel they don't have enough of, and time is something that many of us are not eager to wait for.

We simply want what we want when we want it. This age is one in which everything is available at rapid speeds: food, communication, mail, and travel to name a few. We have been programmed to desire not to wait for anything, to include answers to prayer. Often, we expect God to be bound by the cultural laws of this land—it's your prayer request and you want the answer NOW! But life does not always work like that and neither does God. And there are times when our prayers are answered immediately, but many times, the answer to our prayers will take some time…

Will You Believe?

As we continue on this spiritual journey, we have to be very cognizant to the fact that God gives us the desire of our hearts when we are ready for it. Why would He not? He is an awesome, responsible Father!

So what does any of this have to do with peace? Consider, when you are faced with a seemingly insurmountable life experience and you pray, you naturally want things to turn around in the twinkling of an eye because it's hard, it hurts, and it is uncomfortable. Likewise, if the answer or the relief doesn't come right away, we become anxious, and we doubt God. However, when we are waiting on the Lord, faith is a must. We can't afford to be anxious. We can't afford to doubt because there is nothing that is too hard for our God! Praise God in advance, and expect Him to move on your behalf!

When we receive this revelation, there will be peace. When we put this understanding into practice, the peace of God will guard our hearts and our minds until we receive what we have prayed for. That healing, that restoration, that forgiveness, that freedom… whatever it may be, as we believe God and praise Him in advance, the peace of God will rest upon us and within us.

Peace in the Midst of the Storm

I remember when I was expecting my first child, Maya. I was in the first trimester of my pregnancy, and I was miserable! I'd spent most of this leg of the pregnancy with morning, afternoon, and night sickness. Like many first time mothers, I Googled, read, and inquired about every ache, strain, and tinge of pain that I experienced. This type of homemade "expertise" left me nervous about every little thing concerning me and my unborn baby. So for the first trimester what I feared the most was a miscarriage because it was at this stage of pregnancy when losing the baby was most likely to occur.

With each week that passed, I sighed in relief that my baby was just fine until one afternoon at a marriage meeting. I had discovered that I was bleeding, and so you can imagine, my mind went into overdrive! The last thing that I wanted to see as a pregnant woman was blood. I immediately informed my husband, and we high- tailed for the emergency room.

We prayed together on the way there, and I was silently praying, it seemed, nonstop the duration of the ride. Naturally, we were scared to death. We tried to talk about anything other than what we might have been facing, to include a soccer game that was playing on the TV in the waiting room of the ER. But for as much as I wanted to freak out, I couldn't.

God's presence was so heavy upon me, that I could not help but to be at peace. I knew what the situation looked like, but God had given me a peace in my soul that was beyond logic. At that moment, all of the fear dissipated, and I began to thank God for preserving the life of my baby. Needless to say, Maya is four years old, and she is a happy and healthy child. You see, God is faithful, and if He said it, that settles it; so praise Him in advance for it!

Dear Jesus,

Teach us to place our confidence in You and not in our circumstances, and Lord, we will be careful to praise You in advance.

In Your Name We Pray,
Amen

Food for the Spirit Dessert

Romans 8:6; Romans 15:13; 2 Thessalonians 3:16; Ephesians 3:16-19

Day 20: You've Been Forgiven

What Does God Say?

Therefore, there is now no condemnation for those who
are in Christ Jesus...
Romans 8:1

I felt it necessary to include this verse in a chapter about peace. Remember, we all have sinned and have fallen short of the glory of God (Romans 3:23). This means that every last one of us, from the preacher to the beggar, has missed the mark a time or two.

When we accept Christ into our hearts, this means we chose His will over our own, turning away from sin and turning to the One who saves. This makes you a NEW creation! You are a bona fide new creature in Christ; the old has passed away, and, Behold, all things are new! You... are... new!

Good News!

This is great news! Who we were and what we've done is wiped clean. God has forgiven us, and He has let it go. Unfortunately, sometimes we haven't forgiven ourselves. We haven't let go. We hold on to guilt, regret, and remorse for the sins of our past.

You see, God loves the liar, the thief, the murderer, the rapist, the embezzler, the absent parent, the manipulator, and the adulterer; you name it, He loves them, equally!

He does not weigh sin as we do. There is no scale that says this transgression is worse than another. Sin is sin, period. God, being a Holy

God, hates the sin because it separates us from Him; but He absolutely adores the sinner. Don't believe me? John 3:16 reminds us just how much God loves this *world*. Remember, He gave His best, most precious possession, His son, to have you and I as His own...There is no greater love than that!

Don't allow anyone or anything to take the peace of salvation and forgiveness away from you. When we walk upright before the Lord, we can expect to have a peace within about who God says we are and not the oppression that comes from those who will not let us live down our pasts. So forgive yourself. Don't walk in condemnation another day of your life, for you *are* in Christ Jesus!

Dear Jesus,

Thank you Lord that there is no condemnation to those who are in You! Thank You that when we said yes to You, we've received forgiveness. Thank you Lord for the peace of your salvation.

In Your Name We Pray,
Amen

Food for the Spirit Dessert

Galatians 3:13; 1 Corinthians 1:30; 2 Corinthians 5:17

Day 21: You're In The Will

What Does God Say

Blessed are the peacemakers, for they will be
called children of God.
Matthew 5:9

There is nothing like someone who loves drama. They seem to thrive on it and will find any opportunity available to engage in it. You know the ones…If there is a spark or a flame in the workplace, in your neighborhood, or in your family, they are the ones who are standing in close proximity fanning the flames! Sadly, these people do not bring peace, but instead, they bring dissension and discord. As believers, this is where we come in!

Carry Peace With You

As the light of the world and as a city on a hill, we should carry peace with us wherever we go. Because we live in our neighborhoods, there should be peace there. Because we are employed on a job, there should be peace there as well. When we encounter backbiters, gossipers, and liars, in place of the strife that they are sowing, we should sow peace because we are peacemakers.

Ever been around someone who just had such a sweet spirit about them? Their smile, their words, their deeds, and their presence had the power to cheer you up, calm you down, and bring peace to your personal storm. That's the spirit of God which dwells in the hearts of each and every one of us, as His sons and daughters.

When someone has done you wrong, love them anyway. When you are being overlooked and undervalued, give 110% anyway. Bless those that curse you. Why? Your kindness, your service, your humility will bring peace, and it glorifies our Father in heaven. Remember, the world will know us or should know us by how we love, by the joy we have within that radiates without, and by the Spirit of peace that we carry with us.

Dear Jesus,

You are the ultimate example of how loving those who spitefully wrong you can bring salvation to the masses. Help us to remember who we are and help us to work diligently to represent You in the most reverent way. Teach us to walk like you, talk like you, and love like you every day of our lives!

In Your Name We Pray,
Amen

Food for the Spirit Dessert

Hebrews 12:14; Romans 8:4-5; Luke 6:35; James 3:16-18

Work My Faith
Let There Be Peace

Peace should rule in our hearts. The world should be able to look to us as examples of what peace looks like. It is God's desire that we are always content and complete on the inside regardless of what is happening in the world around us. Peace is just as vital to the life of a believer as water is to the life of a fish! You need them both to thrive! This week's Work My Faith tools will be completely dedicated to helping you to seek the peace that surpasses all understanding and to encourage you to pursue it with all diligence! Again, you can try them all, or you can choose the activity that you feel speaks the most to where you are and what you need.

1. **Heading in the Same Direction:** We all have family members or friends that we keep around because, well, they are our family and our friends. However, when these "loved ones" continue to cause drama, stress, and strain, we have to take a step back and evaluate their role in our lives.

   - Write down the names of all of your dear family members and friends who have caused you more gray hairs than you would like to admit to.

   - Now, categorize these same people into *Have to Keep, Want to Keep,* and *They've Got to Go*. The *Have to Keeps*, for example, would be your parents or your children. *The Want to Keeps* are the people who are not family or may not be immediate family that you want to keep in your life, and, well, the final category is self- explanatory.

   - For those that *you have to* or *want to keep*, you need to begin to set boundaries. Decide what you will tolerate and what you won't. Remember, just because they are your loved ones, it does not give them the right to steal your peace and engulf you in their mess.

- For the final group, *They've Got to Go*, accept that you have to learn to love some people from a distance. This truth is paramount to your keeping the peace within you and keeping peace with what is most important to you.

2. **Leave and Cleave:** Sometimes our lack of peace is self-inflicted. What do I mean? God gives us a free-will. We have the choice to follow His way or choose our own. When we choose the latter of the two, we cause unnecessary drama for ourselves. In other words, we rob ourselves of peace. This exercise requires no journal writing; but, instead, it requires your honesty.

- Are there any areas where you have chosen your will over God's? Is there something or someone that you have placed before Him? Until you put God before those things, you will never have sustaining peace.

- Your assignment: let go and let God! Make the decision today to turn away from the wedge that is between you and God.

- I do know that this is sometimes easier said than done, so focus your prayers to now believe God for the strength to say no to the peace robber and yes to Him.

- Find an accountability partner to help you stick to the decision that you have made for God. Call, text, and visit them as needed to stick to your guns because your peace of mind is at stake.

3. **Praise Your Way Through:** Singing or meditating on the goodness of the Lord and the promises of God brings an unimaginable peace. Find a song or songs that minister to you and sing aloud and/or sing along. It's okay if you can't sing; the Bible says make a joyful noise, right? Praising and worshipping God gives you the opportunity to focus on God and not on your circumstance. Praise and worship draws your heart closer to God, and it minimizes the problem while maximizing the Problem Solver. I guarantee that two or three songs in, the peace and the joy that will well up in your hearts will take your breath away.

4. **Speak Life to Breathe Life:** For this exercise choose any four of the scriptures from this week's Food for the Spirit Desserts and write each one on a Post-it note. Post your scriptures in four places this time that you are guaranteed to see it as you go about your day to day activities. These verses will be this week's scriptural affirmations to help us to live with peace. Again, eventually these scriptures will be committed to memory where they will become our inspirational mantras!

5. **One Body, Many Members:** We have talked about the importance of being united as the body of Christ. This activity will give you the opportunity to do just that! Find an event or a special service that a ministry in which you are not a member or not a consistent visitor is hosting, and come out and support! That's it; it's that simple. However, this small gesture has the power to open the divide that seems to keep us separated instead of united. Remember, as individuals we are able to do some things, but when we are united, we can do anything through Christ!

The Journey Continues

Fruit of the Spirit…

Thank you for allowing me to take this journey with you. When we grow spiritually, life becomes sweeter. Life becomes the abundant life that Jesus came to give us. It should be our desire to grow up spiritually. We can't continue to be beaten up by the trials of life. God has given us power and victory; it's up to us whether we will walk in it or not. Ephesians 4:14 reads, "God wants us to grow up, to know the whole truth and tell it in love—like Christ in everything. We take our lead from Christ, who is the source of everything we do. He keeps us in step with each other. His very breath and blood flow through us, nourishing us so that we will grow up healthy in God, robust in love." (Message Translation).

Just as we cannot stay children or behave like children forever in the natural, truly, we cannot or should not stay spiritual babies forever. To grow spiritually, to mature in our faith, we have to develop the fruit of the Spirit in our hearts and in our lives: love, joy, peace, patience, kindness, goodness, faithfulness, gentleness, and self-control.

It is my prayer that this book has helped you begin to purposely develop the fruit of the Spirit into your life. I pray that you are loving more fervently, that you are filled with joy, and that peace is overtaking you.

Know that this is a lifelong journey. Nonetheless, kudos to you for making the decision to begin! The next two editions of Food for the Spirit will help you focus on the six remaining characteristics of the fruit of the Spirit: patience, kindness, goodness, faithfulness, gentleness, and self-control. Again, thank you for allowing me to come a long for the ride. ☺ Here's to your spiritual growth!

FINAL THOUGHTS

Finally, I do not want to assume that because you are reading this book that you have indeed given your heart to Christ. Please know that Jesus loves you. There is nothing that you have done that God won't forgive if you would just ask. He desires more than anything for you to know Him and to be able to have a relationship with you. You mean the world to God which is why over 2000 years ago, He sent His only begotten son to die on a sinner's cross to pay the wages of sin just...for...you.

What Is Salvation?

Salvation means that when you die, and you will, you will spend eternal life with God in heaven, and you are saved from an eternity in hell separated from God. Salvation also means that as soon as you say yes to Jesus, you are adopted into God's family as one of His children. As His child, you inherit all of the blessings and promises that are recorded in the Bible from Genesis to Revelation. God's Holy Spirit moves into your heart, and you become born again. This means the old has passed away, and Behold, all things are new to include you! Again, you are a new creature with a clean slate in the eyes of the only one who matters: God Almighty.

How Can I Be Born Again?

The Bible shares with us in John 3:16 that "for God so loved the world that He gave His only begotten son so that whosoever believes in Him would not perish but would have everlasting life." The Bible also explains that "everyone who calls upon the name of the Lord shall be saved" (Acts 2:21)! It's just that simple. So, if you're ready to experience real life, allow me to pray this prayer with you:

Dear Jesus,
I thank you for the gift of salvation, a gift that I could never earn and a gift that I
do not have to earn. I admit that I am a sinner. I ask for you to forgive me of all
my sins. Jesus, I believe that you died for me and that you rose from the dead
for me so that my sins could be forgiven. Come into my heart. Be the Lord of my
life. Show me the plan you have for my life, and teach me how to live a life that
is pleasing to you. From this day forward, I am saved, I am forgiven, and I am
yours! Thank you, Jesus!
Amen

About The Author

Bilon Joseph is a passionate educator, author, and transformational life coach. She has made it her life's mission to help others find their own life's passion and to boldly pursue it. Her inspirational writings have inspired thousands world-wide to be the best that God has called and created them to be.

She is the founder of LEAP (Learning through Enrichment and Academic Preparation), a non-profit organization that serves underprivileged youth by giving them tools and strategies to be successful emotionally and academically.

Bilon is currently an English instructor for a local private school. She is also working towards her doctorate of education in the discipline of Reading and Literacy. Additionally, she is currently writing her debut novel, *Sojourner: The Women Behind the Pew* as well as a marriage and relationship how to book co-authored with her husband, Sherman Joseph, called *I Do, What Now?*

To find out more about Bilon's books, Blogs, and personal appearances, you can contact her at:

Phone: (352) 682- 6976
e-mail: bilon@bilonjoseph.com
Website: www.bilonjoseph.com

Also, for daily inspiration to motivate you to Be God's Best You visit:

www.facebook.com/BilonJosephFanPage
www.twitter.com/BilonJoseph
www.youtube.com/BilonJoseph

www.ingramcontent.com/pod-product-compliance
Lightning Source LLC
Chambersburg PA
CBHW021938040426
42448CB00008B/1125